Business Command Center

The Ultimate Strategic Weapon

Roger G. Lewandowski

iUniverse, Inc.
New York Bloomington

The Business Command Center
The Ultimate Strategic Weapon

iUniverse books may be ordered through booksellers or by contacting:

iUniverse
1663 Liberty Drive
Bloomington, IN 47403
www.iuniverse.com
1-800-Authors (1-800-288-4677)

ISBN: 978-0-595-53204-9 (sc)
ISBN: 978-0-595-63263-3 (ebk)

Printed in the United States of America

iUniverse rev. date: 02/19/2009

Table of Contents

I. The Business Command Center 1

    Holding Action First 3

    Necessity is the Mother of Invention 5

    Master Business Plan 8

    Summary of Holding Actions 11

II. What is a Business Command Center 13

    Key Points of the Circulatory Management Chart 17

    Special Points 19

    Circulatory Management 20

III. Business Command Center Leadership 23

IV. How Do You Organize Control of the Command Center? 30

V. Summary 35

VI. Epilogue.. 43

Introduction

This book was written as if I were having a personal conversation with you. Therefore, I was not looking to make a large book with frivolous stuffing for more pages. I wanted something simple and straightforward. I wanted the material to be enjoyable to read, in a timely manner.

I have given a skeleton for you to flesh out. Depending where you are, financially, will influence how much of the early portion of the book you will use because you may already use lean manufacturing.

My comments on lean manufacturing are purposely minimal. I want to make you aware of the tools, but there are hundreds of books on each one subject you can easily obtain from the internet.

I am giving you a road map to be reviewed. I also want you to rethink your business, regardless of where you think you are financially. If you have not reviewed your core strategy, objectives, and mission statement in the past three years then I urge you to rethink them. Put them into today's environment, and see if they are what you need to be successful. I feel strongly 75% of you need to rethink your business and make significant changes to be competitive in today's market.

I wish to highlight the following points:

I. Propose a holding action plan to hold off your competition while you are rethinking your business.

II. Rethink who you are and what type of business you really are. Perhaps, you will see it is time for a change.

III. Rethink your objectives, mission statement, business plan, strategies, and tactics.

New Approach- IV. There are exciting and revolutionary changes in the concept of management that will allow you to outthink any competition.

New Approach-A. "Circulatory management" is a powerful reconstruction effort to flatten your organization and restructure your team.

B. A "new" management concept will make your team powerful and successful. This concept is the "wingman" theory.

C. You are now ready to maximize on your flexibility. A business command center will be the umbrella that will bring a significant break though in management. You will have a powerful and highly flexible team. However, management will bring everyone together with monitoring of the market place twenty four hours a day and seven days a week.

D. I put in some unique operational changes that I want you to consider in your analysis.

1. I want to bring management into a direct role. I want to allow management, which I call the director, to have more time to focus and manage their operation.

2. I also want to have new people present in the command center so they are more accountable and available for quick action. Safety, quality, and distribution are only a few examples of work for the new people. This will focus their efforts and give the directors more time to focus on their primary objectives.

3. I added an entirely new position to report to the business command center called "Competitive Intelligence Gathering." Too often in our day to day life we tend to operate on an internal mode without considering the competition and how they may react and how we should act in return to their changes.

E. A new concept of managing the business command center detail will include three screens for control purposes. Each screen will show unique information to review at the command center meetings. Rather than tying up top management with presentations, I suggested a screen manager to be responsible for collecting all the information needed for the daily meeting.

These screen managers will be responsible for collecting and presenting the agreed upon details for each screen. This will save a large amount of management's time.

V. In order to assist you, the appendix is a reference to detailed information, is key to your success. If you have questions or problems with the detail, then I will answer the questions for you or refer you to several key books available in the market.

Summary

My overall objective is not to entertain you but to challenge you to think about the kind of leader you are. Are you a follower or a bold and passionate leader who wishes to make significant changes? Changes are needed to be a survivor during a brutal part of world history which will be unfolding during turbulent times.

Although Toyota cars are recognized as the leader in innovating tools and lean manufacturing, American cars makers are very successful. American car makers meet Toyota standards are the best car manufacturers. However, Americans must invent a new way to beat Toyota. I believe if you read carefully, then you will discover I have given you the "secret" to exceed all competition in your marketplace.

Americans are known for imagination. We will be tested as individuals, as corporations, and as a country. Be not defensive to what you have but instead be bold to what you can be.

Good luck and good hunting

Roger Lewandowski
World Competition Consultants
CEO

Roger G. Lewandowski founded World Competition Consultants in 1993. As a former president of Carrier Air Conditioning in Canada and Carrier's Residential Heating and Cooling division, he set new records for profit and market share figures. Roger is a recognized turnaround specialist, a member of the National Turnaround Management Association and the author of <u>Successful Leader's Secrets</u> and <u>The Revolutionary Manager's Handbook</u>

World Competition Consultants
1940 E. Lamar Alexander Parkway
Maryville, TN 37804

The Business Command Center

The world is rapidly changing into a very competitive capitalist's world where all countries want to be industrialized to make any product to sell in the world market. In the past, we have been protected by two large oceans keeping possible danger from our shores. Today, with the invention of new technologies and new transportation options we are no longer safe from competition.

Also, the increasing appetite of all humans wishing to increase their standard of living has resulted in the development of an undeclared but competitive war to make products before other countries where rates are as low as ten or fifteen cents an hour.

These people are trainable, and even though there have been some quality problems, they are rapidly correcting them. They are learning to do things with our technology that they purchased, which took us a century to learn and develop. They are turning around and picking up the capability to compete with us in only three to five years. We will see this war escalate and it is going to be a very personal war for everyone involved, the same as a physical war is. We will not hear the crashing of bombs and the people being killed, but there are certainly causalities taking place. Today, we are already feeling the effects of this world competition, and many executives have become casualties as well as thousands of factory workers. Their jobs have been eliminated or moved over seas. These people are the "walking wounded," who are having a radical shift in their living standard. This is only the beginning of the world competition. I have preached for years, all business is war and only the believers will survive. This is becoming true even faster than I suspected, and we as Americans are going to have to change our designs and processes from traditional methods to beat the competition and compete with their lower costs. More intelligent and simple designs using less labor they must have outstanding quality and service ability. We must have a quicker response to all customers' needs and the foundation we must build is outstanding in everything we do and in every step of our process from fool proof design, tooling and manufacturing. This must also include the office work force and their response to customer's needs with systems and processes. It will be possible for them to provide customers products faster than their competition.

China's emerging population, which made great strides already, is in excess of 1,321,000,000 million people. India is the other giant with a population in excess of 1,129,866,000. These two giants, India and China, are eating natural resources of iron, steal, copper, aluminum, and = at a shocking rate. This is compounded by the world's need of oil and coal. In the near future, there is also going to be a shortage of food and clean water as the population grows with better health care and the next world war may be fought for these basic resources.

The governments of China and India face a dangerous treadmill. The more people who receive the material gains then there will be people who are now jealous. In addition, which is extremely important to recognize, this worldwide appetite for material luxuries and the invention of TV globally for all to see is going to put countries that cannot compete into a precarious situation. Politically, it can end in international revolutions or war because of jealousy and greed.

Therefore, China and India accompany other countries that are feverishly going around the world to buy all the raw material and oil they can, or the corporations who produce it, because they fully realize the risk of their political instability if their people become dissatisfied. This will compound world competition in all businesses. There are going to be numerous unhappy losers in the competition.

My purpose is to set the stage of the present and coming world revolutions in business and in all of its supporting needs. All the manufacturing processes and raw materials must be changed radically because of what I have just reported to you. The scarcity of raw materials is so very serious. In addition, major processes and organizations are going to make dramatic changes to reduce product cost. Everyone will have to adapt to a new way of doing business in order to be able to compete and survive in this new world situation.

American present manufacturing is generally stagnated, and while the computer is a revolution, its speed and capability is exceeding our capability to really analyze all the data being generated today. The salary force is suffering from overload. Targets are being missed because there has been little attention given to competitors now competing around the world for the same limited market.

While we address surviving, we must also take time to recognize the fact that what we need is a holding action against competitors. They are at our business gates until we can develop a new approach to manage our business to beat the competition in the marketplace. This means we must do two things at the same time. While we are focusing on surviving today, we must also take time to rethink our objectives and strategic plans to give us the wining edge.

Holding Action First

Here are some thoughts to consider for your holding action:

I. You focus your attention on the 20/80 rule to buy time with the people and processes you have in the market. The principle of the 20/80 rule says that 20 percent of your customers equal 80 percent of your volume. You must concentrate on them and ensure that you are giving them excellent service and quality. For now, if you can have superior quality to your competition then people will be willing to pay extra to acquire that. The Toyota car strategy is successful in that people assume the quality is better and will pay more for a Toyota car. In addition, you will see this in used car lots; people pay more for their cars, which is a powerful marketing advantage perception. We can help your team make this analysis and plan actions.

II. In the office function, we developed a unique concept called Zero Based Process Mapping. We take the old-fashioned idea of zero-based budgeting and combined it with process mapping. Our point is rather than improve processes, which may be obsolete, we better evaluate the process using the zero based budgeting technique of asking, Why need it to begin with? We have adopted the Japanese technique, asking why it is needed five times. This is not to be cute. However, the Japanese patiently unpeeled the onions, so to speak, and discovered the core reasons for decisions. The result may be that you reinvent the process and in doing so you can eliminate several processes in the system and eliminate waste and time. I will not go into more detail, but in the appendix, you will see our pending copyright approach, and it is free.

III. You will notice in item two, I mentioned process mapping for all office functions such as sales, marketing, engineering, accounting. I hold the opinion that this is where process mapping needs to be. As I said, you will find the detail in the appendix interesting.

I found it shocking but true that Toyota does not use process mapping in the factory. They use, as their core tools, Kaizen events. They continue to improve their processes as an ongoing weekly routine. Improvements are made almost continuously.

The new concept called ARK gives accelerated returns on Kaizen, which will help many businesses, be more successful. I wish to implement this process because I noticed many of our clients spending thousands of dollars of money plus employee's time training all employees on what Kaizens events really mean and how they are accomplished. This is performed many times in large training rooms to familiarize them with this tool. In fact, in the basic one-on-one book on Kaizen, it says training is the first step. It is an accepted practice.

1. The retention percentage, after they leave the room, and when asked questions of what they heard were less than 50 percent. As time goes by and they are not part of a Kaizen team, the retention factor falls even further. We found this to be true with corporations who had local colleges put on classes for several weeks. But, in fairness to the colleges, we experienced the same results in three to four hour employee training sessions. Also, as people quit or retire, you need to retrain replacements; this is not normally done in a structured way. Seniority affects the movement of people within a company; this training is lost in the process. If you don't use it, then you will lose it. *See appendix for the brochure explaining ARK further.

Necessity is the Mother of Invention

My company had a recent experience with a corporation, who had three factories, and they were in very serious financial times. It was very important to act quickly. I suggested, based on our experience, they do something different from the normal Kaizen training and implementation.

1. I suggested they have a plant-wide meeting in order for our team to inform their people we will help the team be more competitive. We then came and implemented lean manufacturing techniques to reduce the cost quickly to stay competitive and survive and encourage the employees' cooperation.

2. Our seasoned specialist made a quick, walk-through analysis and determined what processes need to be addressed to see the quickest and greatest returns.

3. He then made a simple process mapping change on a flip-chart and received input from supervisors while the employees proposed changes.

4. They immediately took action to make the change and removed all waste with Toyota Seven Wastes of Manufacturing. *See appendix for free copy.

5. As a result of the changes made, fewer employees were required. Based on seniority; the extra employees were removed immediately. The extra employees went into a labor pool and were used for special projects or replacements due to attrition.

6. This action resulted in the customers knowing what their costs really were.

   There was seasonality in their product line, and at that time, we reduced the labor pool based on seniority and in the future, they will continue to use this practice. If you do not have a seasonal product, then you might need to make immediate adjustments using seniority as a guideline for action.

7. We did not properly record what was accomplished for history. We now require:
   a. A simple case study form for each task to identify what has to be changed and why.
   b. The time started and the time completed is charted on this form.
   c. The cost to accomplish this task is recorded
   d. The forecasted savings is recorded. ROI (Return on Investment) is determined by the client's CFO or designee. *See worksheet in the appendix.

I think the use of ARK (Accelerated Return on Kaizen) is the most realistic and practical approach for Kaizen events today. Thousands of dollars are not lost on training and the time to accomplish it. The results are tracked weekly to prove the savings are there. I can tell you this process was a breakthrough for our clients. The client is now beginning to see daylight because his prices are now more competitive and his sales are now up.

I believe you should consider this as an option. Again, for informational purposed only, if you see the appendix then you will see the worksheet and approach that I am suggesting and you are free to use it to be successful.

This approach is not an expense. It is a guaranteed savings!

One might initially disagree with me on this approach and suggest we use process mapping in the classic Kaizen events. Our clients need fast action to survive today. I am confident that using the ARK approach is the most practical and realistic approach for accelerated cost savings and method changing.

I agree for large planning projects, such as factory moves or total factory reorganizing to velocity flow manufacturing, process mapping must be used.

IV. You should explore pull systems, working closely with SMED to dramatically reduce set up time to customers and processes by at least 50 percent. Look at this option very closely. If you are not familiar with these tactics, please refer to the appendix, where there is further information.

V. You should also be acquainted with using the tactics of Strategic Kanbans to compliment your pull strategy.

Kanbans are a powerful method to eliminate sales forecast and discontinue MRP (material requirements planning) used in planning purposes for tooling suppliers and volumes. You can not survive in a day to day operating using the paper work of MRP because it is too cumbersome and does not accept changes.

You can use strategic Kanbans as a very effective weapon in the market place, for example, build to order products.

A. Have instant delivery capabilities to customer's that have 20 percent of the products that represent 80 percent of your customers

B. On the 80 percent of products that equal only 20 percent of your business, you can establish Kanban inventories on long lead time purchase products and give to customers a maximum of two weeks delivery on build to order items.

C. Set up suppliers on a 24-hour maximum delivery schedule where needed or authorized Kanban inventories for their long lead time components is critical. They must supply you with quick delivery.

D. You can accomplish all of these features with actually less inventory dollars than you have now because you will have inventory flowing rather than being built to forecast and stacking in storage areas.

E. This strategy of strategic Kanbans, along with the dramatic reduction of lead times and using SMED as a tool, can be extremely powerful tools to help create additional sales because of the quick delivery capabilities. Again, the appendix has more details on Strategic Kanbans if you wish to read them.

VI. All of the above improvements can be considered underneath the umbrella of continuous velocity manufacturing, which simply means materials will flow quickly in a non storage environment until shipped. There will be no fixed storage or extra handling. More information is available in the appendix.

Master Business Plan

While the previous tools should physically be considered to implement buying time in the holding action, we must develop a new master plan of new objectives and strategies to be implemented over a three year period. There will be various segments we will discuss later, but there must be a total consistent quality on all objectives and these actions must be achieved first. These major decisions by management cannot be taken lightly. Management will have to demand excellent quality in everything being done in the office and factories through shipping to customers. There are no exceptions to ship anything less that 100 percent quality on your products. Management will be tested because the hourly and salary employees have heard the stories on quality before and seen the management's decision to overturn quality decisions to take care of a customer's needs because the product is useable even though it is inferior.

This discipline by the employees in the office and the shop must represent high quality. It may cost a loss of money or daily shipments. It will disturb the customer when you do not ship the products. This is why management must be serious before they make the statements that many managers have made in the past. The employees must understand any violations by management or employees on quality are terminal. Unfortunately, many employees from management may have made the mistake of authorizing shipments and often feel they had very good reasons to ship. There are no exceptions, and those who violate the quality rule must be terminated as examples. Otherwise, other employees will not believe management is truly serious.

The customer in today's world will pay additional money if they truly receive excellent quality and dependable service. Quality is the first building block, not only for the holding action, but for all future actions. I mentioned the perception of Toyota making better cars than American car makers. However, the consumer does not know the cost of building a Toyota car is actually cheaper than an American made car. This is not reflected in the selling price of a Toyota car because their margins of profit are also higher than GM, Ford, and Chrysler.

We have now established quality is truly number one in all objectives and your strategies must support it.

I believe your business plan should only be an eighteen-month plan because of the rapidly changing technology and competition. The objectives should be fixed and only an act of God or some extremely significant change can occur to make any changes. You must have a firm foundation to build your business on.

Your business plan should be for eighteen months. You must make short term changes in the tactics to compete with competition where necessary. I chose eighteen months for the business plan to take away pressure of only having a one year business plan to have continuity and stability with less planning pressure.

In developing the business objectives and strategies from scratch the very first question you should ask yourself is; "What business are we really in?" This should not be taken lightly because the whole structure of your new strategic plan will depend on your answer.

You must establish your mission statement. Here again, this may sound simple, but there should be considerable thought made by your team, so the employees and your customers understand what your mission really is. The mission statement is not changed at all because it is the foundation on which you build your entire corporation plan and future. It should be short and easily understood by all your employees. Care should be given so you stay in the boundary of the mission statement objectives and strategies agreed upon.

You next objective is to establish what your core objectives and strategies. Everyone must be responsible and understand them the objectives and strategies. You tactics of implementation must reflect the options established to accomplish the core strategies.

These core strategies will continue for your eighteen-month strategic planning because they cannot be accomplished in one year. There must be a continuance until they are accomplished.

The powerful core strategy must be taken seriously to protect the greatest asset you have is your people both hourly and salary. You must always respect them and be fair with them and continue to build trust both ways between you and them. This action should be done on a daily basis. Anyone who misbehaves according to employee conduct rules whether they are, hourly, salary, or management, must be corrected quickly or removed. Whichever is the case, no exceptions can be made. A weary team cannot afford the negative presence of having losers on board. You will discover employees who practice the codes of behavior will generate new ideas and make you successful.

Everyone must be on the team including hourly, salary and management. Everyone should be listened to for the betterment of the company and in solving problems. Management should reward those who make outstanding contributions. They should be made publicly, acknowledging their contributions to the team.

Managements should always study the needs to make the hourly and salary teams more powerful by giving them special training in each of their unique areas. Money invested in training your team will be returned many times over by their continued updating of processes and procedures you already have. If you do not maintain core strategies then policies and procedures will become obsolete as technology and conditions change continuously.

Money spent on capital equipment, after it is installed, is initially used at top quality and efficiency. As it is being used, then it will begin to have less capability and dependability because of poor maintenance, use, and wear. With training, your hourly and salary will now increase their new skills and they continue to increase new contributions to making the total team successful.

Therefore, management, who thinks capital spending comes first over training, is missing a very important point. Top management should ensure the budgets they have sufficient training money. This money should be spent on improving the present systems and abilities not just "nice to have "experienced seminars off campus. This means the Humans Resources area has the responsibility of contributing to the continued success of the corporation and must continue researching new training concepts. In many cases of the past, HR has not been empowered or financed properly to do so.

Summary of Holding Actions

At the beginning of this book, I tried to influence you to quickly adopt suggestions I mentioned for a holding action to defend yourself against domestic and foreign competition. Opportunities that reduce cost and waste will energize what I call a holding action. That means, taking certain actions will buy you time to rethink your business. I say that because, if you are operating under the same strategies and objectives, you were two years ago, then you are already obsolete in today's market place. Like a sinking ship, you begin to see erosions in profits and market share. The suggestions I made about various actions were not meant to give you an in depth lecture but every single item, such as pull systems, Kanban systems, and reduction of waste as a whole, have many books already written about them. My writings were meant to stir a curiosity to explore the various tools available in today's world. I want you to find the ones that fit your product and your culture at this time of transition. As we went through the various choices of action and supporting data I referred you to the appendix to familiarize you with some of the tools. I did the same thing in respect to the strategic planning that needs to be rethought. There are objectives that must be made to achieve your business plan that are semi fixed in execution, where as the tactics to implement the strategic objectives are flexible in the real time world of what is happening today. I emphasized some key points I would like to have you consider as your rethink your strategies, objectives, and tactics. I would like to remind you no company or corporation is better than their people. The most profitable investment you can make is upgrading the people you feel can contribute to your success with the proper training needed. Reward the believers and quickly remove the unbelievers.

The human resources area should be the oil that makes all of the parts of the organization work. In today's world, it too often becomes a political department. By many people's standards, it is more of a necessary clerical function.

However, that is far from the truth. Unfortunately, Human Resources departments are often overlooked by the perception. I urge you to invest more in the human capital than in capital equipment because the human capital will multiply your return with new expertise generating new ideas, and will be one of the critical factors in waging your war. The war will mostly be with multi-national plants overseas.

We can now proceed to address some exciting new concepts, bold and original to not only make you competitive, but patriots for your country. It will make others follow you and regain leadership with a can-do spirit!

What is a Business Command Center?

I have spent needed time with you on the developing a holding action needed to buy you time in the real world to which develops the process of what business you are in and what objectives are needed in tomorrow's world to be successful and the needed strategies and tactics that should be considered to achieve the objectives.

Once you have accomplished the background, fundamentals, and the foundation of your reinvented corporation, then you are ready to take this total reorganization and put it into what I call the ultra strategic weapon for business. I have named it the Business Command Center.

First, let me state where we are before I get into the details of what a "command center" is and "how will it operate."

Our present organizational structures are being used by practically 100 percent of corporations and companies. The organizational structure represents the chairman of the board and the CEO at the top of the chart. Beneath them, in descending order, are the various divisions and their hierarchy being used today.

I have tried to research the origin of the organization chart. The best we could find is it may have started with the Roman Empire. The Roman Empire grew so large with its legions of armies; there was a difficult problem of changing it from a mob into a highly trained specialized fighting machine. Their command structure was written down and used to function as an organizational force in the world at that time. We, in the industry, have carried on with the descending order charts and graphs showing organization structures and responsibilities in the same way the Romans did. The only part we have improved upon is the ability to create new organizations, faster, with computers and communicate from runners to the computer and internet capabilities. We still have this obsolete organization that needs to be rethought in order to be less cumbersome, less of bureaucracy, and a flatter organization regardless of its size is not only powerful but also highly flexible to the real time needs in the market place, today.

We have seen, over the years, many of the innovations in the armed forces are adaptable from military to commercial areas in processes and technologies. In past military days, runners were depended on to communicate between various commands as to what was happening and what should they do. They were then able to switch to cavalry troops. The military kept improving the communications and in more modern times the more various staff functions were brought closer to the firing lines of combat to help collect reconnaissance and intelligence to send to command tents in World War One. In WW2, some of the more advanced commanders were in the German army because they had large vans with communication telephone lines and radios to follow behind the German panzer tanks speeding through enemy lines. The allied commanders took over hotels and key buildings as command centers and tried to have all of the communications come there to find out what was rapidly changing in the battlefield. They were able to gather intelligence quickly. In the chaos of war, many of the hard decisions were crucial happened at the front by commanders, who were bold and aggressive. This holds true in business and war.

One of the blessings of computer technology is electronic inputs needed to send or receive could be utilized by the computer.

In business, we too must know the enemy. The top three competitors need to be determined in the business command center. I will talk about it later on, but there should be an individual assigned to know everything about the top three competitors to receive feedback from the field sales people and dealer's updates on their activities.

Are they aggressive? Do they have new marketing programs? Are they having problems in the field with quality?

Include any other important information in real time that can be fed back by the sales people or dealers via e-mail or direct contact. This individual, male or female, should be recognized in the corporation as your expert on the top three competitors. They should use the assistance of everyone and put together a confidential report that states the strengths and weaknesses of the competition verses the strengths and weaknesses of your management team product wise, service wise, quality wise, and price wise.

These competitive information specialists should always be the sounding board of what the competition might do to counter the action you intend to take. As I talk later about the command center and responsibilities, we will come back to this person.

Strategically, this competitive input of competitive strengths and objectives should be used as input for the tactics you want to use to make your strategies work.

This completes your holding action need. You are now ready to move into the Business Command Center.

The Business Command Center

1. We now have the foundations and tools ready to insert into the business command center. We must now use them in their proper place the same way we would put a puzzle together. They must fit the total picture in the overall organization culture.

    My road map changes the total organization design into a totally more effective total team.

    Let us first pause and review what we have today. We have generally been using the "Roman Army organizational structure" of how they controlled their legions from a mob into a precise delegation of culture with the various layers reporting through channels to the very tap.

    This basic management structure has continued over thousands of years. As our information society has exploded with the use of computer software. We are overwhelmed with information internally externally in corporations. Management's answer has been to create an even larger bureaucracy with new levels of new titles to handle the information explosion.

2. Another result of bureaucracy in management has added a corresponding explosion of meetings that resulted in middle management spending at least 50 percent of their time in meetings with another 25 percent of this time preparing for them leaving them only 25 percent of this time to communicate with management and their people. This leaves them little time to be innovative.

    The result is not only ineffective management but the communication time needed to answer key customers questions is delayed. Valuable counsel is also lost for the key customers.

    Working long hours and leaving less time for family is the only band aid for middle management. In many cases they begin to develop health problems and disfunctional marriages. The wife in many marriages feels as though she cannot compete with her husband's work.

    Success is a very demanding mistress and the more time you give her the more time she will demand. We have reached a critical point in the use of time. We all know the right meetings are critical in any business. I believe the total structure must be replaced using the business command center as the overall umbrella. It cannot operate effectively using the old traditional organizational structure. So, we need to implement a new organization that I call **"circulatory management."** All disciplines will be reporting equally to a business command center. This will flatten the organizations and focus emergency attention on their responsibilities in the command center.

I have illustrated this in a new organization chart I have named **"circulatory management."** This concept will result in a total team concept. Each component has its own title used in management. I do not want to get into what titles are used, so I will call all management a director except for the CEO and CFO.

Key Points of the Circulatory Management Chart

1. I have added some positions to the command center traditionally subordinate to the director's position. Examples for your organization would probably be quality, safety, and warehousing.

   It relieves some responsibilities from the director's position and allows them to focus on their key responsibilities.

2. By having these positions report to the command center, they are more exposed and can directly contribute to command center needs. Their tasks will also be quickly accomplished.

3. Most of the competitive intelligence comes from a new position. It is not listed to any other team. If the information is used correctly, it interacts with all of the support areas of the organization. All of the support areas must begin to think about what their competition is doing and if they can do better. They may also steal ideas from the computer.

   In order to direct this position, he or she must be a part of the command center. However, they will report to the marketing director to receive directions.

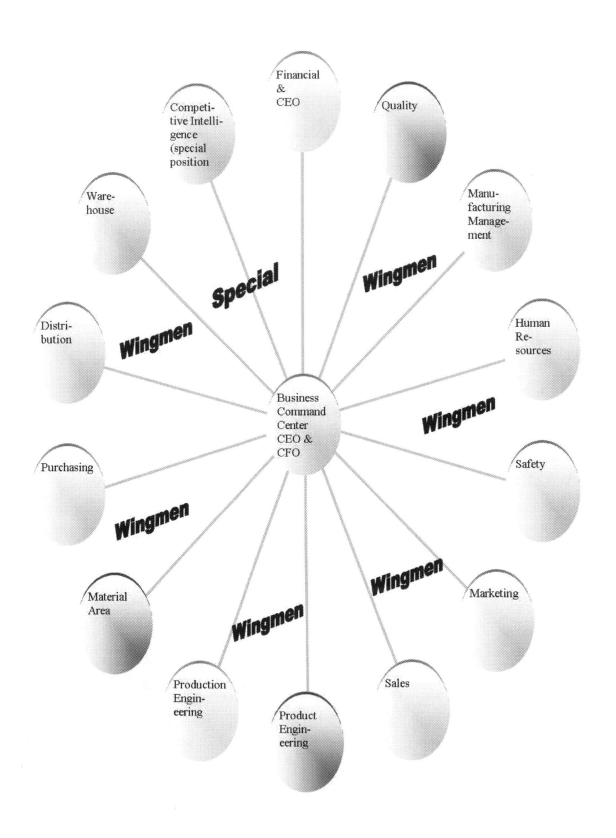

Special Points

1. The financial department represents the CEO, who's wing man is the CFO at the center of the command center.
2. Competitive Intelligence will report directly to marketing in a subordinate role. It will not have a wingman, but it is very important to the overall command center because it is listed as one of the activities.

Circulatory Management

Circulatory Management is a method to flatten the organization. The object of this new concept builds a team that is highly focused and will respond quickly to any opportunity or problem.

Everyone will be responsible to execute their function, but no one will have their own personal agenda. Too often in business, a personal agenda will get in the way of team work.

The key leaders will bring the command center together. They will be exposed to peer pressure and "visibility." They must have the needed facts available to contribute to team results.

I do not think the old fashioned organization can support the control center concept because leaders are no longer kings of their own world. They are now team players.

I am not naive to think that circulatory management will stop internal politics.

At the same time, I am also introducing another new concept to the organizational chart. You will notice a connection bar on the organizational chart that says "W-man" between two regularly competitive positions.

In order to further push the team concept, the connecting "Wing men" is an idea from WWII. In the early days of WWII the United States saw tremendous casualties when the pilots were in combat. They operated as the pilots did in WWI because they acted as individual pilots. They fought to survive and become Aces.

The United States Air Force developed a better way of fighting enemy planes. They divided the pilots into two-man teams, so in combat a pilot could attack the enemy while the other watched the other pilot's back. The new concept became know as the "wing-man". This concept was extremely powerful and successful. It is still being used in present day.

Adopting this policy will give every director a wing man to be successful. Every director will have agreed on objectives from the leaders of the command center. The CEO and CFO will be the team commanders.

The team will be judged professionally by 70 percent of their objectives. 30 percent of their judgments will be from helping their wingman accomplishing objectives. Now they have a meaningful and financial reason to work as a team. All bonuses, stock options, and other fringe benefits will depend on accomplishing objectives agreed on with the CEO and CFO.

There will no longer be internal competition between individuals. However, as the pilots did in WWII, they will become best friends. Their success will depend on the success of others. I believe the secret to making the command center a powerful concept is to destroy old concepts, so there will be no other choice but to make the new concept successful.

When the Roman Army was conquering the world, they tried to invade England. However, there was a lot of grumbling and fear within the army because the English had a new weapon called a cross bow. This revolutionary weapon could kill from a distance which made swords less effective. The Roman Generals told the captains of their ship to "burn the ships" after the troops were on shore. That meant their only option left was to successfully conquer England. Consequently, they were successful in doing so.

The key to making this total concept successfully extends from leaders having the passion to improvise where necessary in order to make their tasks work. They must beat their competition to survive.

"Burn your ships," and move on to victory.

Business Command Center: Leadership

The command center will be managed by the CEO and CFO as a team. They will make all final decisions based on inputs presented to them. The CEO and CFO will be like conductors of an orchestra. They will not play the instruments but instead direct everyone to be on the same song sheet! (Action plan)

There may be occasions when one of the commanders will be required to be elsewhere. In their absence the one remaining part of the team will be empowered to make all needed decisions in all major discussions. This may occur if one of the directors is not available for the daily meeting, then the designated leader will make the decisions. No one is indispensable in the new organization. The CEO or CFO must make the final decision. They can be contacted on conference telephones as needed. Therefore, it is critical for a telephone number to be available to reach all the teams.

The command center meetings should not last longer than a maximum of two hours after the major items have been agreed upon. There may be special reports and update presentations made that will not require all the disciplines there. Once the critical updates and key decisions are made, the directors can request a meeting using the command action for their own department. As you implement the command center you can adapt it to your culture and business.

1. Financial (CFO) – the financial report should include:

    A. The overall financial years to date profit versus forecast on line charts showing the last year's actual profits for the same period and the sales year to date. The current year should also be on the chart.
    B. The charts should reveal the total budget forecast of expenses versus actual expenses.
    C. There should be a review of the departments who are over budgets. It should show the budget versus actual amount of profits. The director of the departments must explain their reasons for being over budget and the corrections made.
    D. Make sure the chart includes a summary of the overall year to date expenses as a percentage of sales. On the line chart, the ratio of the expenses to sales?

E. Any other financial charts that the team deems appropriate to be reviewed plus any key points the financial director wants to make or question that need to be included.

2. Quality: suggested key items are as follows

   A. The shipping quality as a result of audits ready to ship units to customers needs is a necessity in the chart.
   B. Include the actual warranty dollars versus budget.
   C. Display the warrant dollar costs as percentage of sales. On the line chart include last years warranty dollars percentage of sales.
   D. What are defect sales internally on key process? List the major reasons for them.
   E. Any key information the quality director wants to pass on or question.

3. Human Resources

   A. What is the general morale of the hourly workforce and the salary workforce?
   B. What are the key concerns the human resources director has?
   C. What is being done to address further education of the workforce?
   D. Are there any concerns about OSHA or environmental issues to be addressed?
   E. Are there key relationships with the community that should be reviewed?

4. Warehouse Director

   A. Is there a backlog in the warehouse of shipments to be made?
   B. How much cycle time is needed from the time of receivable at the warehouse until the product is shipped.
   C. What is the dollar value of inventory? Is there a certain amount that is obsolete? If so how much is it worth? What are the SKU's involved?
   D. Who are the carriers and what is their cost today verses the past two years?
   E. How much space is being used for warehousing? If there is more than one, list the locations and the space available. Are they rented or owned? What is the cost per square foot for each warehouse?
   F. Are there any other problems or opportunities that should be discussed?

5. Director of Distribution-

   A. Review the list distribution locations. Be careful to include their address and size.
   B. Is it a privately owned distribution? If so, who are they and where are they located? What selling dollars do they produce? Who are the customers they work with? Are they dealers or a direct, one step distribution center?

C. Are there any other problems or information that the Director of Distribution wishes to communicate?

6. Director of Manufacturing-

   A. What is the status on the yearly budget verses the actual expense on the line graph?
   B. What is the manufacturing strategy? Is it a one shift, two shifts\ or partial third shift operation? How many hourly and salary personnel are involved?
   C. The Director of Manufacturing is in charge of the in process fabrication inventory. What are the total dollars and the inventory turns? What are the budgeted dollars verses the actual dollar amount? What is the budgeted inventory turns for fabrication verses the actual amount?
   D. What are the lead times needed to be competitive in order to use speed as a competitive weapon in the marketplace? What is the lead time for customers in days?
   E. What is the completion production rate verses the forecasted rate?
   F. What is the actual (not adjusted) delivery percentage verses the customer's request?
   G. What are the other key areas the director wishes to discuss?

7. Director of Materials-

   A. This position is separated and reports directly to the command center because of the major impact to material costs. They must be aware of the opportunities and risk in working with overseas suppliers.
   B. What are the purchased parts inventory dollars that are tired up? How do they relate to the budget? What are the inventory turns as related to the budget?
   C. How many suppliers do you have? Using the 20/80 rule, which are the suppliers that are in the 20% that equals 80% of the volume?
   D. Are you using Kanban controls to reduce lead times? What are your key lead times with suppliers?
   E. What special programs do you have for the supplier's talents that involve design?
   F. How much time is being lost due to lack of purchased parts? The objective should be 99% on time delivery so that production schedules can be met.
   G. Are there any other key areas or assistance the Director of Materials needs help with?

8. Director of Production Engineering-

   A. The Director of Production Engineering combines the classic Industrial Engineering responsibilities with the traditional Manufacturing Engineering capabilities. This gives the director complete flexibility and accountability for all production processes.
   B. What new processes are being investigated with product engineering?

C. What is the status of production tooling in regards to age of dies and fixtures? Is there a need to make updates with Industrial Engineering's help?

D. The Director of Production Engineering is also responsible for all Kaizen events with the use of the Industrial Engineers and the strategic use of Kanbans. What is the current status of these and the objectives?

E. Are there any other key areas or assistance the Director of Production Engineering needs help with?

9. Director of Product Engineering-

A. The Director of Product Engineering is responsible for the innovation and design of products that marketing needs for the marketplace. He or she will work closely with marketing and sales' input.

B. They must also work closely with Production Engineering to continually improve the capabilities and flexibilities on tooling.

C. They must be aware of all of the new material designs to reduce the materials cost as much as possible. Working closely with Production Engineering, they must try to reduce the significant amount of parts needed to put into the product in order to reduce labor cost.

D. The director has to work closely with the materials area to assist suppliers in conforming to the standards they established.

E. This position is very important because it involves input and work with practically every discipline on the command center. The leader must be innovative, passionate for success, a team player and people oriented. It is not an easy position.

F. Are there any other key areas or assistance the Director of Product Engineering needs help with?

10. Director of Sales

A. A line chart showing the actual sales year to date versus the budget year to date should be used. On this same line chart, different colors should represent last year's sales and profits.

B. Include a chart showing the 20/80 rule on customers so we can identify where the key customers are from with a team standpoint and discuss how we can give them outstanding service.

C. Working with the competitive intelligence director, closely, you should identify your top three competitors and list their weaknesses and strengths compared to your weaknesses and strengths. Discuss what can be done to exploit their weakness with your strength while addressing defensives. Address what needs to be done to strengthen your weakness.

D. Are there any other key areas of assistance the Director of Sales needs help with?

11. Director of Marketing
    A. Show a line chart depicting the share market from year to date verses the forecast. On the same line chart show what your actual share market is verses the forecast from last year.
    B. A review of the organizational structure of sales verses their key competitions would again be accomplished with the help of the director of competitive intelligence.
    C. Marketing gives the entire business the direction to accomplish the objectives agreed on. They should be responsible for the pricing function.
    D. Marketing should work closely with a director from competitive intelligence to understand what the real street price is and propose a strategy on pricing.
    E. The marketing department, with inputs from the marketing director, sales director, and the competitive intelligence director, should work with the product engineering director in the design of new equipment to be competitive in the market place. This should include a target cost with a new product and input from the quality director. The new product needs to be the best quality in the market place.
        The product must not only perform outstandingly, but it should also be easy to service. It should set a standard for excellence and life expectancy.
    F. Are there any problems or opportunities that should be discussed with the command center team?

12. Director of Safety
    A. I have listed the Director of Safety as a separate director reporting to the command center because it is critical send your people home in at least the same shape to came to work in. You must have patience to watch over your people as a guardian of the workforce. Safety can be a key factor in the loss of personnel needed when they are injured. That could have a negative effect on production and particularly on quality to our customers, which is paramount.
    B. Also important, are injured employees that can cause serious financial problems. Highlight their positioning and importance not to be subordinated to some other area such as Human Resources. HR is a critical function for the employees. I see them working closely together as a team.
    C. When visioning the command center, I see a line chart showing the lost hours that have occurred because of safety and a record of current status accidents. The same chart must include where were your company was last year compared to the current date.
    D. The Director of Safety should give us an overall report of areas he is concerned about and where he needs assistance. This should be done to remove any hazards, quickly. The other support team in the overall command center should report on how they are going to make corrective actions in their areas.

E. If any employee's injury causes lost time, then the supervisor is responsible for employees in the office, shop, or field, must report the injury in the command center meeting as to why the accident occurred and what is being done to correct it.

F. I believe the position of the Director of Safety reporting to the command center gives credence to the fact our team members and employees are our greatest asset. They always have priority over anything else being done.

G. Include any items to report or question by the safety director that have not been covered.

13. Director of Competitive Intelligence

A. This is a new position reporting to the command center because as it is in combat, we cannot act without considering what the competition can retaliate or effect our operation. In today's world of world competition, it is even more important to find out how we can compete against the enemies. I believe the position should consider the following.

1. Working with Marketing and Sales as a team, agree upon what your strengths and weaknesses are verses the top three competitor's top three strengths and weaknesses. You must give your inputs and considerations to the business command center as they review the objectives and tactics.

B. Competitive intelligence should develop a field input on competition from your sales people in the field plus your customers in the field and the dealers and distributors you have in the field. They should issue a report on the top three competitors as they get feedback from their field of contacts. There may be come radical change that should be brought to the attention of the command center about a new competitor or something dramatic happening to other competitors that are beyond the top three that the command center should know about.

C. This should be a highly confidential summary status issued monthly to a very select group of directors, mainly sales, marketing, product engineering and of course to the commanders of the business command center.

D. Any strategies or marketing considerations that are new should be run by the competitive intelligence director to know what reaction might come from the field.

E. The director of competitive intelligence should monitor the pricing in the market place by competition and any intelligence they can gather to know the lower price by the competitor because they are in trouble on cash flow or overstock inventories. This should be shared immediately with marketing, sales, product engineering. If something dramatic should occur then it should be brought to the attention of the command center.

F. The Director of Competitive Intelligence should be able to bring any topic to the table he feels is critical to the recommendations of the business command center.

We have reviewed my suggestion of directors and who should attend the daily management control center meetings. I include input regarding what I feel are core contributions by each director to the command center. You and your team will need to determine the best service for your team's style, culture, and business.

How Do You Organize Control of the Command Center?

1. Finalize the topics you wish to review daily and the format of who goes first in the organization meeting.

2. Establish a daily agenda of priorities be covered first because they are important. The screen managers will review key points with the CEO and CFO the day before meeting for special instructions.

3. I believe there is a critical need to better manage the control center using three separate screens. There is so much detail that you should cover, and having three screens and screen managers will add to better control over what is being done.

4. **Having control of the data in real time furthers the importance of having three screens and three screen managers.**

The employee in charge of each screen totally responsible of the topics assigned to his or her screen. The screen manager needs to have all of the updated information readily available at the 9 AM start of the meeting. He or she will individually coordinate their screen and handle the presentation in the control center. The directors must give priority to the corrections or the information needed for the following morning's 9 AM meeting in sufficient time so the screen master will have it ready for presentation. This way, the director's valuable time is not wasted on training the presenter.

Each screen manager will have people on three shifts reporting to them separately. He or she will collect all information from the field and throughout the corporations. Their screens will be filled with important information for the following day.

It is important for all the directors to understand their obligation is to supply timely data to the screen managers. Each director is responsible to see that his people conform and have the necessary support for the following day. This must include the special action they suggest be taken, by whom and when. Each screen manager will have an assistant reporting to them to take daily notes of the action that needs to be followed up and help expedite needed information. The screen manager's portion is critical because it becomes an each director's responsibility to support timely action.

5. I suggest a first class telecommunications conference call system be included in the command center and also a first class recording machine that can pick up all of the conversations through speakers. The recording should be available in a library inside the command center for reference as needed by the director.

6. The command center must have security so only a limited amount of people are allowed in with their directors when needed. The security should also consist of a limited number of keys to access the command center. A security person will be available to allow a director into the command center for information updates twenty-four hours a day.

7. My next topic is the design of the command center itself. The space I am suggesting could result as a consequence of Kaizen events or a reduction of inventory. The location of the command center will vary with each corporation and their desires.

8. The floor plan should be a separate building beside the first floor of the factory being the command center. I recommend the building consist of a second floor to house the computers. I am suggesting there be one for each screen for a total of three. They are totally independent of each other and feed data down to the command center. The second floor holds the people on three shifts collecting the necessary data and receiving communications throughout the field as intelligence coming in. The detail from the field is a result of what the command center wishes to receive, but the more up to date communications that are in real time then the bigger advantage you will have for using speed and flexibility as a competitive weapon 24/7 in real time.

Special Note:

As you break down the bureaucracy, by the central use of the command center, then you should have quite a few salary head counts you do not need. The command center will eliminate at least 50 percent of the meetings taking place. Therefore, you should be able to have adequate head counts to man the command center's three shifts.

First Floor Layout
(Rough design, layout needs to be developed by team)

Small Office Quiet Room	Screen I Information (1) Field operation (2) Sales (4) Pricing (3) Marketing (5) Actual to forecast	Screen

Screen

Screen II Information
(1) Quality
(2) Production

(3) Materials
(4) Human Resources
(5) Product Engr.

(6) Schedule

"Command Table" will have individual microphone to speak to group and field people when on conference calls inside

Screen III Information

(1) All financial
    actual to budget
each discipline.

(2) Percentage to
    sales
(3) Actual to forecast
(4) Job to be done

Screen

"Examples only"
Develop your own priorities,
adjust as you gain experience
Notice I suggest key grouping
together, i.e., field operation,
sales and marketing data one
group for better control.

Small Kitchen And Rest Area

ENTRANCE

Women's And
Men's
Restroom

Second Floor
(layout needs to be developed by team)

Second Floor Purpose

(1) Assign a leader for each screen. They are responsible to maintain computer and data input of their screen.

(2) They will have separate computers and storage for their screen.

(3) They must be responsible for all communication needed to update data 24 hours a day and seven days a week.

(4) They will need support people to accomplish this objective.

(5) Communication links will need to be established with the correct directors to maintain real time data for their screen.

(6) Management must develop the "dashboard" approach where condition "Red" receives first priority at meetings. On major specific items, condition yellow will be reviewed to avoid reaching condition red.

(7) Screen leaders will be at a 9:00 A.M. meeting each day and present their screen update and answer all requests on specific data and capability to roll over to detail that supports presented data.

```
Small
Kitchen
And
Rest
Area
```

```
Women's
And
─────────
Men's

Restroom
```

Summary

I tried to have you think out of the box. I offered various suggestions and strategies as examples that you may consider in the:

A. Holding action to allow you to have time to rethink the business.

B. Approaches to consider in your rethinking of your business mission statement, objectives, strategies, and tactics that you need to develop.

C. I also introduced you to the revolutionary organization concept to eliminate loss time in the bureaucracy.

D. In doing so, I have also introduced you to the concept of circulatory management, which eliminates internal squabbling between various directors. They are normally in conflict over their objectives in a business situation.

I introduced you to the wing man approach. There was a copy of a WWII situation, where fighter pilots flew in pairs to protect each other in the success of the mission.

I have paired up internal division of directors. As an incentive to work together to complete both objectives, I am suggesting 70 percent of an individual's director's measurement be on completion of his own objectives, but 30 percent of his competition is on his wingman's objectives. Therefore, a natural team spirit can be built between two naturally competitive individuals. The chemistry from them working together will bring a mutual financial gain.

We elevated certain positions of the directors to report to the command center that are normally subordinate in the old system. We added a new position I believe is critical called "competitive intelligence". It is listed directly on the circulatory managements chart to accent actual to reports to the marketing department as a subordinate. It will have full visibility and participation at the command center. It will be a resource for all directors to gather information on the competitors. This will not only work for sales and marketing strategies but also for cost and design of products, distribution, knowledge on the key leaders of the competition and so forth. I believe the lack of the position in the past has cost proper actions being taken.

I also organized a new concept I referred to as a "screen manager". This person is totally responsible to insure the information is available on the screen detail for the daily 9 AM meeting. Again, I emphasize that all directors are going to be held accountable for their screen information. It must be available for the meeting.

The critical concept of the command center stems from everyone being trained to do their job and support the screen manager, who's only responsibility, is to coordinate and pass on the information that the directors or their people give them. The director stands responsible for his own area at all times.

E. A reality check at the end needs to be made. It may not be practical or possible to have the CEO and CFO present at every meeting because of their other responsibilities to the board and the customers. I suggest there might be a given day of the week where the structure is for them to be present to handle the major decisions. In the absence, they will have a subordinate fully authorized to take action on what is needed on that day and cannot wait.

In reality, there may be occasions when several directors cannot be available for good reasons. They too must have empowered subordinates at the meeting to make decisions. In my opening comments, I mentioned that business is war, and war cannot just be put on hold until somebody shows up. The team at the command center must always take action in real time. After management has taken out the bugs in the system, there may be abbreviated portions of the meeting on serious problems. They could occur over a teleconference connected to the key decisions makers so they can be alerted by the command center.

The command center is a real time, living organization. It can be used throughout the day for presentations from management after the initial structured meeting is complete or for reference information.

Lastly, all of these tools are meant for management to rethink what you want done and how it should be done. I have tried to do give you a skeleton for you to flesh out to management for your organizations specific needs. I want this to open your eyes to the future of what can be accomplished. I see this as only a foundation of what the future will be in laser light communications and responsibilities. There is too much information being generated from throughout the world. I believe it is beyond the control of one individual. At some point, you will have to revise the structure for key items to be focused on. A danger becomes prevalent in today's business world when management is expected to cover too many areas and therefore it ceases to become an expert on all areas. That process leaves the danger of bad decisions and poor timing or no action but reaction to the combat of daily operations in business. I hope I have energized you to look at the different possibilities and adapt them as you see fit while maintaining the base of a command center after you have completed all of the homework that I have suggested. **You must outthink your competition just not outwork them. If you only operate computers on ground rules then you will surely lose.**

I want each of you to win this war. I want to leave you with the Marine Corp's orders.

Apply as needed:
I. Improvise
II. Adapt
III. Overcome

Good luck and God speed.

WHAT ARE THE BENEFITS OF HAVING A BUSINESS COMMAND CENTER?

1. Decisive and timely action will be taken in "Real Time."

2. Dramatic reduction of meetings.

3. Speed will be a competitive weapon.

4. All discussions in Command Center can be recorded for follow-up and historical records.

5. All employees will be better prepared and more visually responsible to have needed information available when required.

6. The total team will be focused on the command center instructions and needs

7. Productivity will be improved, dramatically.

8. As in war, you will be continually under attack. Do not play defensively, but with all the timely information, you will be able to outplay them and beat them in the market place.

9. Reward the believers and remove the non-believers.

Future Possibilities

The following is what I call "continuous improvement" (Kaizen):

1. We will use the dashboard approach to set priorities in our presentation.

2. In order to give the key executives flexibility to travel and still be accountable for the Business Command Center, a portion of the command center's key decision makers can be brought together at a certain time and may be teleconferenced to the executive that is in the field.

3. The command center meetings will always begin exactly at 9:00 AM. They should be planned so they will conclude by 11:00 AM. If there is an emergency requiring more inputs in the field or someone else, then these will be exceptions to the time of 11:00 AM and will extend to whatever time is necessary to resolve the decision making.

4. The command center should be used for making presentations requested by the command center leaders after the conclusion of the command center's business for the day.

5. The screen managers, as I said earlier, are responsible for the data that is being presented on their screen. After the full presentation, they must maintain the follow-up and prepare the inputs for the following day's meeting. They must split the tasks among the different team members according to responsibilities.

6. The screen managers, using the dashboard approach mentioned earlier, will work with the CFO to establish the objectives be used for the dashboard to run the business, which simplifies the amount of items and accents the critical items.

   The screen operator is responsible for key data for the screens, and the work in working in real time. If one of the measurements goes in to red or completely missed the target, the operator must alert the team members to identify the problem in a quick manner. If the command center leaders are not directly available, then they must be located. The leaders must give their final approval before an action is taken.

7. A spin off of the command center may be a video conference with the full organization or other management teams at the same time with the customers.

Epilogue

"I would be delighted to coach or assist you on a journey where man has never gone before. We must embrace change and lead it to where we want it to go; otherwise it will overwhelm us and destroy us."

Roger G. Lewandowski
CEO
World Competition Consultants
865-681-3844
Roger@wcconsultants.com
www.wcconsultants.com

Roger G. Lewandowski founded World Competition Consultants in 1993. As a former president of Carrier Air Conditioning in Canada and Carrier's Residential Heating and Cooling division, he set new records for profit and market share figures. Roger is a recognized turnaround specialist, a member of the National Turnaround Management Association and the author of Successful Leader's Secrets and The Revolutionary Manager's Handbook

World Competition Consultants
1940 E. Lamar Alexander Parkway
Maryville, TN 37804

Appendix

1. Process Mapping

2. Toyota Wastes (pictures)

3. ARK Concepts

4. SMED

5. Strategic Kanbans

6. Operational Due Diligence

7. Supply Chain Management

Zero-Based Process Mapping Analysis

"If you have to do it, do it right!"
Turn a problem into an exciting opportunity!

This approach will not only save hundreds of thousands of dollars, perhaps millions (depending on the size of the study), annually on your cost and fringe benefits in your salary rank but will also negate the crude and risky knee-jerk reaction of just naming a percentage for every department to cut.

Our Zero-Based Process Mapping Analysis is unique in the industry. Based upon normal process mapping, most consultants map the old processes and make the agreed upon improvements. However, we have found in just mapping, you run the danger of simply improving an obsolete process. Based upon our experience, we first justify the process. Is this process even needed? In evaluating processes with their users, we are able to eliminate many obsolete processes and in some cases invent one new process which will replace several old processes. We always insure the user is comfortable with the revised process because they are the ones that must maintain it.

This process will justify itself and its cost by removing all of the accumulated hidden waste (unnecessary salary people) that has taken place over the last few years.

It will reduce the timeline to get the processes completed giving better reactions to problems as they occur and better customer service.

The removal of all marginal people in the processes needed and replaced from the excess salary more-skilled employees adds a tremendous amount of productivity to the entire process also. New spirit, ideas and enthusiasm take place.

"This approach should be communicated to all the salary people as a need for being competitive and the survival of the organization."

Zero-Based Process Mapping Analysis

© Pending

Zero-based process mapping analysis is a professional alternative to arbitrarily reduceing salary head counts. Instead you go through a process analysis which will determine if there are extra headcounts and where they are in the process. Therefore, in the final analysis you will not have voids and confusion you have in making an arbitrary reduction.

In this process, you will end up with an organization which is leaner, more nimble, and will be energized to move more quickly, with more enthusiasm, and lastly, eliminate marginal employees.

We will simplify the approach we use into measured steps.

I. We need to first review with the senior management person to see if there is a possibility of combining positions, eliminating positions, and identify any marginal people that he has in top management.

    The reason we need to start at the top is once management has agreed to their people being acceptable, any changes we might recommend will now have a strong foundation to begin our review of their organization. They will be our key advisors.

Our next step is to begin the process mapping analysis.

This will be the entire salary group below the top staff (which the top management person has already evaluated).

We will start with a given discipline which is reporting to one of the staff's senior managers. We would use his organizational chart as our guideline of his staffing. As we said earlier, he will be a key advisor, and we will report to him on his areas.

One example might be accounting. We will track and map the entire salary process step by step from the first step in the process. Again, we will be mapping every salary headcount reporting to this senior staff person. We will do the same process for every other senior manager's staff based on their organizational chart.

C. We will map the process in the following individual person's detail:

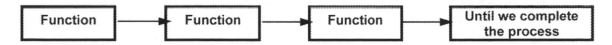

We would reach an agreement with the person on what their function is.

We would determine if that function was really needed by asking "Why?" five times, as the Japanese suggest, to make sure we reach the core answer after examining the alternatives.

Should it be changed?

Could it be combined with another function?

Requirements and procedures change, and there is normally always an imbalance between functions time-wise (not everyone has an eight-hour workload). Many times, the variants are down to a 50 percent workload. By balancing the workload, we can reduce waste and eliminate salary headcounts once we reach an agreement with the key advisor (management staff person).

      6. A new job description is written based on the analysis of each function.

A "dual mapping" must be kept for analysis and presentation. In other words, a before-mapping and after-mapping summarizing the reduction of excess people and reduction of a timeline again from before and after of each staff area summarized in headcounts and timeline reductions.

    IV. As we are able to eliminate or combine operations for the purpose of this analysis, you will mentally put these people aside in a holding position.

    V. All managers must evaluate their employees' performance in a descending order of performance. The best are at the top with the marginal at the bottom.

       The steps taken in Item I through Item IV identify people who are now excess. They would go into a "theoretical holding pool" of manpower. The managers will then, as a team, take excess salary pool and across the organization agree on the best place to use them in eliminating marginal employees. The results will be an increase in the caliber of the total team and the elimination of waste (salary

headcount) that can be laid off. This will make a significant impact in saving cost and increasing the caliber of the total team and reducing timelines.

VI. You must now address the span of control of middle management. By eliminating the excess salary people, we will find certain supervisors or managers that now have only two or three people reporting to them.

Management must now determine if they can combine functions or responsibilities and eliminate certain managers.

VII. You would again use the approach we did with salary and put our total middle managers in descending order of performance. Then evaluate the excess managers we have against the descending list and replace them with better qualified people. These managers who are no longer needed will join the salary people who are also no longer needed to be removed.

VIII. **Once this is completed, the senior staff should get together as a team to see if they can now eliminate levels of management and become more of a flat organization. Here again, the managers are evaluated and the least qualified are expendable or if needed replaced by a new hire that is more qualified.**

Conclusion

Our mission is not to eliminate people; our mission is to eliminate waste at every level and help management reinvent their organizations, using speed as a competitive weapon.

We as outside people have no vested interest, nor are we politically involved, which are obstacles in many organizations.

We will update your processes and job descriptions from what is currently being done and eliminate all waste.

We will have formal timelines, mapping, charts and what is being done in each step of the functional process as an audit in the future and, perhaps for the first time, have documentation of what really happens in an organization that management does not really know.

The end result is that you now have a new, exciting, motivated "lean team" that will have ideas and challenges and achieve greatness beyond your expectations (save millions of dollars in cost and benefit in the process).

P.S. You eliminate the "terrible risk" and major morale problems of just assigning a "best-guess layoff percentage."

TOYOTA SEVEN WASTES OF MANUFACTURING

Transportation

Overproduction

Motion

Process itself

Inventory

Waiting

Making
Defective
Products

JAPANESE SIX-S's

1. Simplify
Keep only what is needed

2. Straighten
Organize all needed items in
a standardized fashion

3. Shine
Clean up the workplace

4. Stabilize
Maintain and improve the
standards of the first three S's

5. Sustain
Discipline to maintain
established procedures

6. Safety
Keep the environment
and people safe

Accelerated Return on Kaizen (ARK™)

We have noticed that many of our clients have spent a great deal of money and employee's time training their employees on what Kaizens events are in training-room situations to familiarize them with this tool. In fact, in the 101 books on Kaizens, it relates training as being the first step. It is an accepted practice.

We have studied this with several of our clients after the training has taken place, and found the following negative results:

1. The retention percentage, after they leave the room, and we ask questions of what they heard was less than 50 percent, and as time goes by and they are not part of a Kaizens team, the retention factor falls even further. We found this to be true with corporations who had local colleges put on classes for several weeks. But, in fairness to the colleges, we experienced the same results on our three to four-hour training.

2. As people quit or retire, you need to retrain replacements; this is not normally done in a structured way.

3. As seniority affects the movement of people within a company, this information (training), again, is lost.

Necessity Is the Mother of Invention

We had a recent experience with a corporation who had three factories, and they were in very serious financial trouble. We suggested, based on our experience, that we do something different than the normal kaizen with the training.

1. We suggested that we have a plant-wide meeting, saying that we would come in and implement lean manufacturing techniques to reduce cost quickly to stay competitive and survive and we encouraged the employees' cooperation.
2. Our seasoned specialist made a quick, walk-through analysis and determined what processes need to be addressed for the quickest and greatest return.

3. He then made a simple process mapping change and received input from the supervision and showed the employees proposed changes and asked for their input.

4. They immediately took action to make the change and removed all waste (Toyota Seven Wastes of Manufacturing).

5. As result of the changes made, fewer employees were required and based on seniority; the extra employees were removed immediately. The extra employees went into a labor pool and were used for special projects or replacements due to attrition.

6. This gave us a better idea of what our costs really were for sales. There was seasonality in the product line, and at that time, we reduced the labor pool based on seniority and in the future, they will continue to use that practice.

7. We didn't properly record what was to be accomplished, in my viewpoint. We now require this:
    a. A simple case study form for each task to identify what's to be changed and why.
    b. The time started and the time completed is charted on this form.
    c. Also, the cost to accomplish this task is recorded
    d. The forecasted savings is recorded. (Return on Investment, ROI)
       (See worksheet attached.)

Summary

I think that the use of ARK (Accelerated Return on Kaizens) is the most realistic and practical approach for Kaizens events. Thousands of dollars are not lost on training. The results are tracked weekly to prove that the savings are there. I can tell you that this particular client, not because of this alone, is beginning to see daylight because his prices are now more competitive and his sales are up.

ARK

Case Study

Client: _____

Location: _____

Objectives

_____
_____
_____
_____
_____
_____

Results

_____
_____
_____
_____
_____
_____

Time/Date Started_____   **Time/ Date Completed**_____

Estimated Cost _____ **Estimated Savings**_____ **ROI Savings** _____

Remarks_____

Name_____

SMED

One of the outstanding tools of lean manufacturing

SMED means "Single-Minute Exchange of Dies"

But also Welding Set-ups and actually any set up used in manufacturing

- SMED is one of the most overlooked tolls in the lean manufacturing gold bag

- SMED can make your total process more competitive and increase your profitability quickly

- SMED is a Japanese tool to reduce setup; it is powerful because it does not cause you to spend capital money. It help you utilize the capacities you already have today

Here are a few of the advantages

- You can increase the utilization of your plant capital for equipment, and often avoid spending millions of dollars on new equipment.

- You can eliminate all overtime.

- You can reduce lead times for products by 50%.

- Using SMED, we can reduce run sizes and cycle the product quicker, giving you greater flexibility to take care of customers.

- Eliminate large inventories because you have gained capacity and you can cycle the inventory faster.

- Less storage space required.

- Fewer inventories mean less carrying costs.

Strategic Kanbans

Kanbans are normally thought of as a modern way to control inventories. They replace the old fashioned use of reorder points and max/min systems in controlling inventories. The truth is, Kanbans are misunderstood and misused many times.

I believe that the proper use of Kanbans goes much further than controlling inventories and I'll just share with you some thoughts. Each one could be embellished in quite a bit of detail. But my thought, to you the reader, is to plant some seeds on how to use Kanbans strategically. So I will use these bullet thoughts as a skeleton for this conversation.

1) It is difficult in today's world to make a forecast that is accurate in building products for the marketplace. I would say that in most forecasts, you are lucky on an annual basis if you are 75% correct — unless you peg the marketplace to build the quantity you wish. The danger is that you limit your growth and your capital utilization. **The key point is that forecast for production should only be a guideline for planning capacities, but not a build schedule.**

2) If you accept the fact that forecasting in unreliable in today's world and could seriously impair your cash flow, you can use finished goods Kanbans strategically for your build and sales functions. A few key points:

   You use the 20/80 rule and evaluate what your most profitable and best sellers are. These are the items you should ship with 24 hours for a competitive advantage. You set Kanban quantities up that build in the replacement time for the Kanbans, plus an original safety factor, which will be fine-tuned as you use this tool.

   You now can see what your maximum inventory dollars will be as you begin to build on these Kanbans.

   One of the exciting advantages of using these Kanbans as a strategic tool, the way WCC uses it, is that every time a Kanban is reaching a replenishment point, we demand that the marketplace be evaluated quickly to see which way the trend line is going (up or down) for requirements of your product. So you are operating in real time. Too many times, in today's world, when business is increasing, your inventory is too low and when business is decreasing, inventories are too high. You're always behind the curve.

The marketplace is a very volatile environment; it is affected by seasonality, competitors dumping, quality problems affecting sales, pricing disadvantages, and so forth. The exciting part is that if you use Kanbans correctly, you are constantly adjusting the Kanban quantity on finished goods to your best feel of the marketplace. If you do it correctly, this makes you highly competitive without large cash flow problems

3) We have just discussed the use of strategic Kanbans on finished goods for using the 20/80 rule, which states that 20% of the volume is 80% of your profitability.

We now can discuss the 80% of the finished goods items that equal 20% of your business. **You can't carry Kanbans on everything, nor should you** — a classic error by some management. We still want to give our customer the best lead time on these items without having them on Kanbans.

We must evaluate what the items are that make up those assemblies that cause longer lead times, because you want to be very flexible and competitive against your competition, On the purchased items that are used in their assembly — the secret is to get the suppliers to carry the Kanbans and deliver in 24 hours. We may have to assist and train the suppliers as to why and how to set up Kanbans, maintain them, and again, check every time a Kanban is reordered that has the latest information as to its needs.

As a customer, you must establish a discipline for the supplier to report to you that he is, in fact, maintaining your Kanbans.

One of the options with suppliers that you also must consider strategically is that they might have a long lead-time from their supplier on a special part or special raw material. If so, as professionals, you may consent to authorize a portion of the Kanban inventory cost. Again, if you visualize that we are talking about the 80% that creates 20% of the business, the volume should be low until you have done something to shift it to a high volume classification (20% equals 80% of the business).

This is simplistically said, and it's not complex to use Kanbans as a centerpiece of your strategic planning to be very flexible, highly competitive, with control of cash flow. It is exciting as to its potential. You can out-think your competition!

4. We now should address the manufacturing parts. And, again, we should not use Kanbans as just an inventory control tool. We must evaluate all of the manufacturing parts individually and develop a specific strategy for them. Let me list a few of the options to consider.

a) Wherever it's possible — the equipment to fabricate, weld, or even paint should be moved to the point of use; so you stamp it out, you weld it, you paint it, and you put it on the product. Again, it depends on the process needed to finish the part, but technology, for example, has given us the option of mini powder-coat booths for painting. The point being, whatever the process in this design for manufacturing, try to use it as point of use. When I was in Japan years ago, I was surprised to see idle machining equipment in assembly. The Japanese tour guide smiled and said, "We buy used equipment, recondition it, and put it in assembly for point of use, and they would rather have a used piece of equipment sitting idle, that may be for limited parts, than to have the inventory."

b) On large, bulky items, we should arrange the process so that the second shift makes only enough parts to get through the day shift. I call this the "bakery theory," in that they bring people in early to make doughnuts and then they stop for the day. The point is that there must be arrangements to handle large parts differently and minimize the stock.

I recall with one client, we had parts that were 4' x 6' and we ended up putting in a press brake, and we would have what I call the "blanks" in assembly and they would form them as required. **My point is, whatever the situation is, there is a way of simplifying it and having it flow to the point of use.**

5. On the 20% of the manufactured parts that go into the 80% of the volume, if they cannot be manufactured at point of use, then they are eligible to be put on Kanbans.

In doing so, the main criterion of Kanban quantities is the built-in time for replacement with a small safety factor. It is critical that every time a Kanban is to be replenished, it is signed off by a supervisor in the materials area that the MRP trend, or other tracking software, is used to see if the part is going down (due to seasonality) or should be going up.

The biggest fault with Kanbans is that if they are not properly used and limited, you could lose control of your inventory cost. That is why each individual item is strategically reviewed as to how that part is made. Is it a point-of-use item, a Kanban item, or a build-to-order item?

One other option, as you are reviewing the strategic use of each part internally, is to check and see if it makes more sense to purchase that part than it does to manufacture it. We tend to not do this or not to audit ourselves as often as we should.

Conclusion

In today's world of using speed as a competitive weapon and to overcome the fog of forecasting the future, Kanbans are especially qualified to limit your risk; and at the same time, accelerate the response to customer requirements.

Also, one of the benefits of using Kanbans strategically (internally in manufacturing) is that you can avoid the chaos of tearing down setups for rush jobs or a customer's special request. In many facilities, Kanbans eliminate the mass confusion with regards to scheduling needs (the chaos of lost time, overtime, and so forth).

Manufacturing should have their internal lead times shortened to a maximum of three days through the use of these methods. At that point manufacturing lead times can be frozen for three days to avoid all of the confusion of changing schedules in the factory.

I'll close by calling this the "duck theory," in that, as you watch a duck glide across the water, it looks so smooth and easy — but beneath the water, he is paddling his feet like mad to go forward. **In manufacturing, the flow of materials should be like music and the feet paddling is the strategic thinking done to design for manufacturing, eliminate obstacles, and maintain quality in all that you do.**

Roger G. Lewandowski, CEO
World Competition Consultants

WCC's Ultimate Total Operational Due Diligence

WCC's Ultimate Total Operational Due Diligence is a one-of-a-kind concept that you have never seen. We actually turn over every "rock" (function) and see what the <u>real status</u> is; also, very importantly, at the end of each item researched, we write a special recommendation to be addressed on that item.

This results in an amazing one-of-a-kind total operational analysis "book."

Details? – We address at least the **<u>101 items</u>** listed in the attached summary index. We include digital pictures where appropriate to make a statement; we will also include copies of key data that we've referred to as exhibits.

WCC not only provides the most complete analysis that has ever been done on the operational side of the acquisition business, but most importantly, WCC provides all the documented facts for each item. Our clients know more about the seller's facilities than the seller knows because we do turn over every rock in our analysis. Therefore, our clients can negotiate a better price to cover the inadequacies of the existing operation.

In our report, there is a page for each numerical item with the risk rating (no risk, medium risk, high risk) for that item with supporting pictures and documentation.

On that same page, our specialists record their recommendations of what should be done as a corrective action. **These recommendations give our client a jump start on the turnaround.**

When our clients follow through on these recommendations, they **save hundreds of thousands of dollars quickly**. If we are in charge of the turnaround, **we target a turnaround time of two years instead of the normal turnaround time of 4-5 years.**

This is a very cost effective insurance policy to avoid risk on costly purchases. The negotiation dollars that you save from this analysis will pay our cost many times over.

Knowledge is power!
This in turn generates huge profits.

Operational Due Diligence Areas We Address

I. Marketing
1. Identification of customers
2. Identify core 20/80 customers
3. Share of market analysis
4. Strategic plan
5. Review distribution, if applicable
6. Review sales function
7. Strengths/weaknesses
8. Top 3 competitors' strengths and weaknesses
9. New product introduction procedures
10. Check for product proliferation
11. Check product positioning

II. Order Entry
12. Current process
13. Organizational structure
14. Customer lead-times
15. Top 3 competitors' lead-times to customers
16. Frozen Cycle?

III. Product Engineering
17. Organizational structure
18. Test facilities
19. Design for manufacturing (DFX)
20. Service consideration
21. Technical equipment availability

IV. Materials Area
22. Organizational Structure
23. Evaluate computer systems (MRP, ERP)
24. Number of suppliers
25. Number of parts controlled
26. Number of discrete bills of material
27. Bill of material accuracy
28. Review floor operation
29. Special supplier programs for control of "A" items

30. Strategic use of Kanbans
31. Pull versus push?
32. Visual factory techniques
33. Application of supermarket concepts
34. Point of use stocking (POU)
35. Inventory turns
36. Dollars tied up in inventory
37. Dollars tied up in slow or obsolete inventory
38. Supplier cost improvement programs
39. Suppler quality improvement programs
40. Supplier rationalization plan
41. Make versus buy program and policy
42. Standardization program
43. Scheduling
44. Review of scheduling policies
45. Use of TAKT time
46. In-house lead times
47. Safety stock used
48. Schedule reliability attainment
49. Schedule linearity attainment

V. Manufacturing Floor Operations
50. Review of organization
51. Lean manufacturing utilization
52. Identify key processes
53. Downtime and causes
54. Equipment utilization
55. Plant layout
56. Condition of equipment
57. Preventive maintenance programs
58. New equipment needs
59. Productivity measurements
60. Overtime

VI. Quality
61. Review organization
62. Review current strategy
63. Cost of quality measurement
64. Warranty cost
65. Key quality audit areas
66. Supplier corrective action policy and practice
67. Customer support for quality
68. Computer system

69. Capability for root cause analysis (RRCA)

VII. Manufacturing Engineering
    70. Organizational structure and responsibilities
    71. Tooling and fixture design (internal or external?)
    72. Outsourcing program
    73. Cost reduction targets
    74. Projects review

VIII. Industrial Engineering
    75. Review organization
    76. Method of verifying productivity
    77. Use of TAKT time in planning
    78. Cost reduction programs
    79. Projects review

IX. Financials
    80. Cost of all major departments as percentage of sales
    81. Current position of forecast versus budget
    82. Past two years and present year financial charts and data for sales, forecasts and profitability
    83. Standard cost procedure
    84. Review all variances
    85. RONOA
    86. ROI

X. Human Resources
    87. Number of salaried and hourly
    88. Normal work hours
    89. Number of shifts
    90. Attrition/retention rates
    91. Absenteeism
    92. Health care costs and trend lines
    93. Worker compensation obligations
    94. Union/non-union
    95. Status of morale, hourly and salaried
    96. Demographics
    97. Contractual issues to be considered
    98. Safety record
    99. OSHA compliance
    100. Machine guarding
    101. EPA compliance
    102. Recordable injury rates current year and prior

Supply Chain Management

In a classic definition supply chain management is generally described as the entire process, beginning to end, of planning, implementing, and controlling the elements of the supply chain to maximize efficiency, inventory management, and velocity.

These elements encompass all movement of raw materials, work in process inventory and finished goods from the point of origin to the point of consumption or sale.

The idea for total supply management is that no single link in the chain can optimize inventory management and velocity. It takes every link in total collaboration and orchestration to achieve maximum efficiency and return on invested capital.

Thus, supply chain management must include the planning and management of sourcing, procurement, manufacturing, distribution, and logistics. It takes as a given that the coordination and close communication by all of the vested parties is evident throughout the chain.

Generally speaking supply chain management is comprised of three main elements; strategic, tactical and operational.

Strategic elements consist primarily of the strategic location and number of manufacturing and/or distribution centers and the strategic partnership with suppliers and/r distributors and in some cases, end customers as well. Other strategic decisions include the information technology underpinning the supply chain management process and make vs. buy decisions.

Tactical elements involve the actual decision making within the supply chain. These elements can be sourcing decisions and contract formations, inventory decisions on amount, type and location and the transportation decisions regarding frequency and carriers.

Operational elements relate to the actual execution of the planning. These include the daily production scheduling, demand planning and forecasting, sourcing planning and execution, and inbound and outbound execution.

As supply chain management has grown in acceptance as a preferred business strategy the expansion of third party logistic companies who specialize in inventory management and distribution into the main stream supply management is a notable force. Companies have come to realize that these providers offer a tool box of skills that enable them to do these transactions and movements more efficiently and often for substantially less cost than the manufacturer itself may be able to do.

Third party logistics management has been a growing component of the supply chain for a number of years and expertise and guidance they can offer is often very valuable.

There are many notable companies in this field that are extremely efficient and have seen extraordinary growth. UPS, the shipping giant, has one such operation with a myriad of optional services. Another logistics giant, Ryder, also offers comparable services and expertise.

Another element in supply chain management and fulfillment are contract manufacturers for products and companies whose core competencies lie in the design and development of products and technologies. Companies such as Microsoft with its high powered gaming system Xbox and a host of telecom companies rely on these contract players. One such company, Flextronics, has positioned itself in the mainstream of this niche and has grown into a multi-billion dollar enterprise.

Many companies have developed specific software applications to assist in supply chain management. These include broad based enterprise resource planning such as SAP or Oracle and many more specific specialized self-contained products. Communication offerings often include electronic data interchange packages and many web based tools as well.

Successful supply chain management means that communication up and down the chain must have velocity and clarity and these products are invaluable to make this happen.